HARMONIOUSLEE
LITERARY MAGAZINE

LEE HIGH SCHOOL
CREATIVE WRITING MAGNET
2017 - 2018

Cover Art: Graphite on Paper
by Shelby Martin

Contents

Syllogism by Raina Verser..pg.4
    Art: Colored Pencil and Water Color on Paper by Travon Lacy
    Pencil by Favian Gonzalez
The Last Time You Came Over by Colby Meeks.................................pg.6
The Silence by Justin Fleming..pg.7
    Art: Pen and Acrylic on Paper by Carlie Knight
Love Lessons by Shalimar Lacy..pg.8
Kundiman by Ariana Brown...pg.9
Curious by Oliver Gemmel..pg.10
    Art: Tempera on Parachute Cloth by Justin Leake
Drowning by Whitney Baker...pg.11
Packages by Zoë Maddox..pg.12
    Art: Acrylic on Canvas by Anya Madry
Useless Words by Suzānne Drouilhet...pg.12
Façade by Shalimar Lacy..pg.14
Ending by Shalimar Lacy..pg.15
    Art: Charcoal and Paper by Carlie Knight
Forevermore by Kydarra Pope..pg.16
Depression is Opression by Dylan Starling......................................pg.17
    Art: Screen Printing by Kiara Cooper
In Sane by Margaret Buckner...pg.18
    Art: Watercolor, Pencil and Paper by Teylor Atchley
Abandonment by Porche Jamar...pg.20
    Art: Screen Printing by Bradley Marshall
Simplicity by Raina Verser...pg.21
Reclaiming by Natalie Roberts..pg.22
    Art: Marker and Tempera by Caitlyn Hayes
I Love When I Shouldn't by Kydarra Pope.......................................pg.24
    Art: Colored Pencils by Destionna Cooper
Give Me A Chance by Destionna Cooper...pg.26
When The Chips Are Down by Zoë Maddox....................................pg.27
Invisible by Malachi Christian...pg.28
    Art: Graphite by Tiffany Hawkins
Make A Wish by Margaret Buckner..pg.30
    Art: Pen and Ink by Tiffany Hawkins
Gone by Madison Maine...pg.32
Tomatoes by Margaret Buckner...pg.33
    Art: Pen and Ink by Tiffany Hawkins
How To Perform the Perfect Trade by Marko Elmore......................pg.34
    Art: Digital by Eli Davis

Don't Be Ashamed by Oliver Gemmel......pg.36
    Art: Digital by Eli Davis
Elasticity by Shecoria Akins......pg.37
1st Amendment by Kayla Dunlap......pg.39
    Art: Tempera on Parachute Cloth by Grace Lemley
War by Daisha Thomas......pg.41
    Art: Charcoal on Paper by Carlie Knight
Excerpt from Myth Hunters by Ariana Brown......pg.42
    Art: Pencil and Ink on Paper by Grace Lemley
Womanhood by Daisha Thomas......pg.44
    Art: Colored Pencils and Pencils by Coddie Jones
Your Eyes by Bella Garbeil......pg.45
Monster in the Bed by Natalie Roberts......pg.46
    Art: Painting by Isabel Waring
Serendipity by Porche Jamar......pg.48
    Art: Reductive Print Make by Travon Lacey
What it Means to Be A Woman by Iauniss Smith......pg.50
    Art: Colored Pencil by Isabel Waring
Together We Can by Siouxann Juber......pg.52
Excerpt from The Untitled by Ben Watts......pg.54
    Art: Pencil by Isabel Waring
Shackles by Ariahna Battle......pg.55
Gravity by Colby Meeks......pg.57
    Art: Watercolor on Paper by Maegan Buckelew
My Love by David Vieyra......pg.57
Home by Zoë Maddox......pg.58
    Art: Screen Printing by Maegan Buckelew
Thin Ice by Shercoria Akins......pg.59
    Art: Tempera on Parachute Cloth by Gretta Wright
At the Women's March by Maya Glenn......pg.60
    Art: Screen Printing by Nate Tippett-Henderson
Fearful Lover by Suzãnne Drouilhet......pg.62
The Call I Don't Remember by Kayla Dunlap......pg.63
    Art: Screen Printing by Satori Koontz
More Than Human by Keira Folsom......pg.64
    Art: Chalk Pastel on Paper by Jack Clifton
Vampires Smoke Menthols by Kayla Dunlap......pg.67
Grief by Natalie Roberts......pg.68
    Art: Reductive Printmaking by DJ Matthews

SYLLOGISM
Raina Verser

Simple machines are just that: simple, summarized by strings of verbs.
They are beautiful because they are self-explanatory.
Pullies pull. Screws screw. Levers lever.
You may extract numbers and ingenious conceptions if you're curious.
But, at its core, a simple machine is and is always just that: simple.

Suppose for a moment that the human heart is a simple machine,
forgoing romance and illogical compulsion.
The heart pumps blood through your waiting veins until you die.
Then, having accomplished its purpose, it, too, will die.
Witness, folks, the most magnificent love story ever told!
"The Heart that Died Because its Owner Died and its Purpose No Longer Existed"

Do not consider errors of the heart.
The gradual shuddering that lulls you into sleep…
The flutter as you observe wandering flecks of sunlight in your soulmate's eyes…
The metallic shrill and screaming tension as you are seized by fear…
Unnecessary. Lapses in function do not matter because, at the end of your life,
the analogy dictates that the human heart is a simple machine,
that it is and is always just that: simple.

Perhaps the world is easier to digest in this form. It must be less painful
to swallow the words "pulley", "screw", "lever" instead of "death", "love", "terror".
Maybe it is hard to accept that our lives are not the product
of the syllogisms we harbor.
If the human condition is complicated and the human heart is simple,
then life, too, must be simple. Yet it isn't, because the human heart is not and is never just that simple.

THE LAST TIME YOU CAME OVER
Colby Meeks

soup
cold soup
cold soup in a small pot
on the broken stove

soup
cold soup
cans of soup
red: spilling out of a campbell's soup can on the microwave

soup
cold soup
tomato soup in a sun yellow bowl
on the kitchen table

soup
cold soup
spilt on the floor
puddles of red

soup
cold soup
my hands
cold red tomato soup

or was it blood
i don't remember

THE SILENCE
Justing Fleming

His screams are quiet and soft,
but they are aggressive.
Words from his mouth move like the winds of a hurricane,
but he doesn't show his feeling through real words.
He shows them through a disguise that he was never meant to be:
his gorgeous looks and his soft skin,
his blood is warm because it makes up for his cold heart.
He walks around seeming normal and simple,
but his mind is scattered like broken glass because of what people say.
He thought his life was useless but some told him otherwise.
He thought it was time when he couldn't bare to continue playing the game of life,
but when he said he was leaving no one believed him.
So when he finally said it was over,
he didn't even think twice of his actions.
The day it happened no one could hear or feel anything
but the silence he had left behind,
the broken and cold silence.

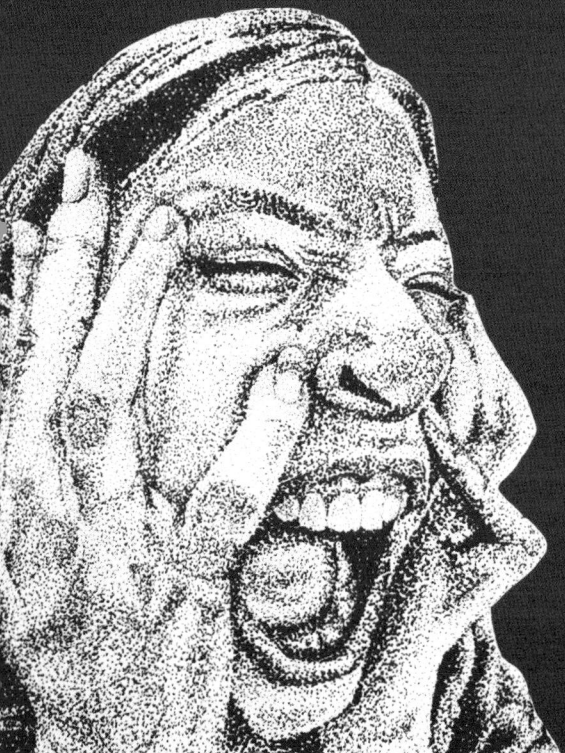

LOVE LESSONS
Shalimar Lacy

The way you teach me to love,
Is like walking down a beach.
It looks easier than it seems.
Like leaves floating down a stream,
It can never be defined,
Until you open up your heart,
and let someone inside,
When you let someone in
Don't push them out again
you'll never know how your future might turn out.

The way you teach me to love,
Is how you hold me in your arms with care.
and run your fingers through my hair
full of love and sincerity
I know you love me
When you kiss my nose instead of my lips.

The way you teach me to love,
when we walk down the street
People stare, but we don't care.
You pull me closer

 The way you taught me to love
Has kept me alive all these years,
The way you taught me to love,
has taught me how to love myself.

KUNDIMAN
Ariana Brown

"Radio music sucks," Osias said, nodding to the back. "I've got a milkbox of CDs back there. Take your pick."

Phoebe reached into the crate of CDs in the backseat and pulled out a handful. "'My Girl,' 'I'm a Believer,' 'Buttons and Bows;' what is this, the 60s?"

Osias kept his eyes on the road. "They're all good songs. Buttons and Bows is the 1940s, though."

Phoebe rolled her eyes as she reached back to return the CDs to the crate. "Got any songs from within the last year?"

"Good music is not conditional to our generation." He reached back and plucked one of the CDs out of her hands before she could put it back. "Let's listen to…" he glanced at the CD as he popped open the case. "My Girl," he said with a wink.

CURIOUS
Oliver Gemmel

I dreamt you were by my side
That you didn't act like nothing happened between us
Now I am just curious
Curious as to why things changed
Was it the way I acted?
Was it the way I spoke?
Was it my insecurities?
Never mind, it doesn't matter anymore
Things aren't the same.
I dreamt of us
We were happy
Where did that go?
I dreamt we lived forever
Nothing could destroy us
I dreamt you were my love
Now you act like I am nothing more than an acquaintance
I dreamt of a life with you
Now there is no guarantee we will still be friends
I dreamt of happiness
Now I struggle to smile
Naturally, at least
Now I am curious if you even care
I'm curious as to why you think I am okay
Why you think I haven't cried myself to sleep
Why you think that your absence is not killing me
I'm curious as to if you cared in the first place
All too curious

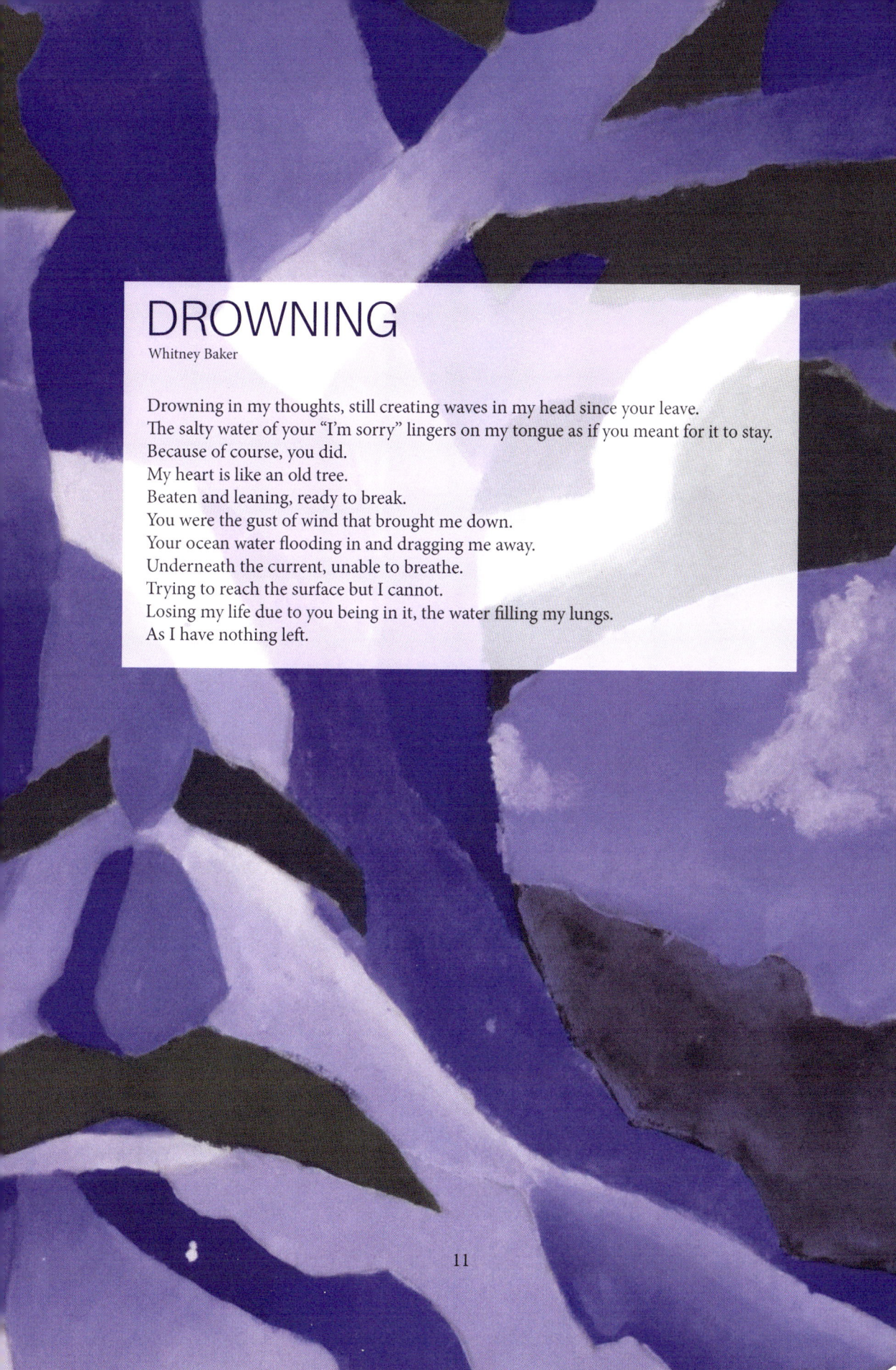

DROWNING
Whitney Baker

Drowning in my thoughts, still creating waves in my head since your leave.
The salty water of your "I'm sorry" lingers on my tongue as if you meant for it to stay.
Because of course, you did.
My heart is like an old tree.
Beaten and leaning, ready to break.
You were the gust of wind that brought me down.
Your ocean water flooding in and dragging me away.
Underneath the current, unable to breathe.
Trying to reach the surface but I cannot.
Losing my life due to you being in it, the water filling my lungs.
As I have nothing left.

PACKAGES
Zoë Maddox

Don't leave your heart on the doorstep for me
Left as a present meant for keeps
I'll forget to pick it up
Like I did with the pieces of myself
That still lay scattered on the kitchen floor
Or the letters from my sister
Asking how I am
Lingering under the bed
Hidden like dust bunnies
It will remain on the porch
Staying out in the pouring rain
The baking sun
And the freezing snow
Because most of the time
It's hard to remember
I am loved

USELESS WORDS
Suzanne Drouilhet

healing hands aren't always the softest
calloused fingertips wipe the tears from my eyes
as worn out arms embrace me
there's a pain in my throat
that keeps me from speaking
if only sobs and cries held
true meaning in our ears
maybe then
we would understand how a soul can ache
because words can only tell us so much
and it's almost always never enough

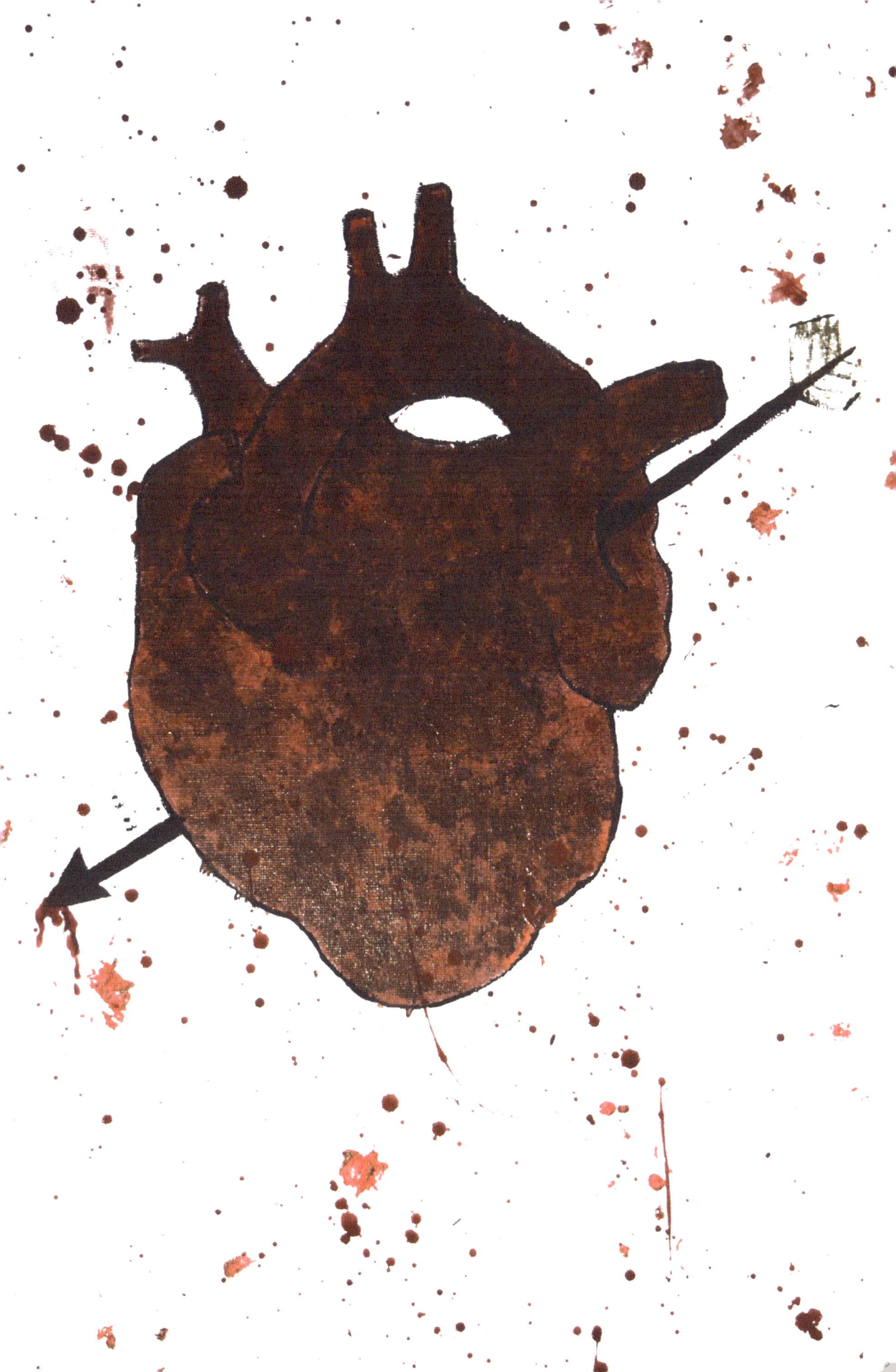

FAÇADE

Shalimar Lacy

My smiles hide secrets no one will ever know.
People do not realize that they aren't real.
They just sit with me and smile.
Without realization.
My heart is nonexistent.
I can't feel the happiness that people see in my faux smile.
I feel only the pain in disguise of happiness.

My smiles are fake.
They are not real.
My soul aches for something genuine.
It aches to come clean.
I ache for someone to realize my pain.

I go on day after day,
With no one trying to find out my truth.
I live in a world of cluelessness.
I'm farther gone than I realized.
I always question myself.
Am I even real?
Because I feel gone.

This is the time.
My time to turn around after all these years.
But how can I when I feel so far away?

My conscience tells me something.
It says 'Everything will be okay'
But then I realize something.

My smiles are fake.
They are not real.
but it will be okay.
Because you're here with me.

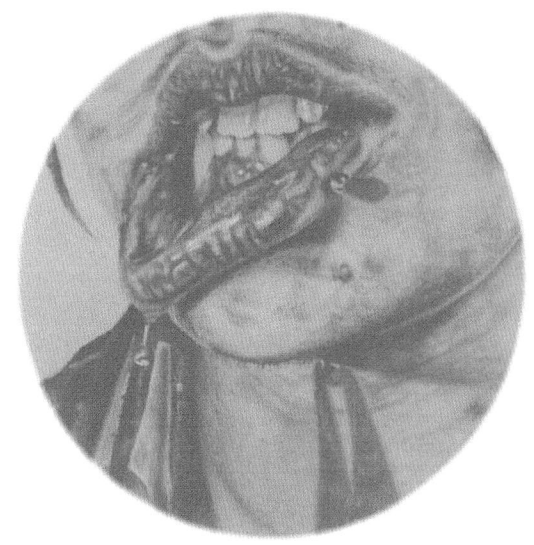

ENDING
Shalimar Lacy

I had not seen the beginning of us
until you kissed me that one memorable night.
I never thought of loving you,
until you devoted yourself to me.
And I fell,
I fell hard.
You stole my heart too quickly
ripped it apart
tore it to shreds
you ruined me.
4 years of loving you,
4 years of abusing me.
9 years of knowing you,
9 years of getting to know the wrong you.
Now down the drain
in the gutter
dying slowly
because of you.

FOREVERMORE
Kydarra Pope

I could never get enough of you,
I need you in my life.
for as long as I live
I want you right here beside me.
not just on the good days.
but on the worst.
on the days where it feels like
we won't make it out alive,
I won't leave from by your side.

I love you.
the type of love
even Shakespeare couldn't express.
the mystery of my loyalty that
even Sherlock couldn't solve.
I want you to be with me
until I can't remember my name.
until I can't remember my past
until I can only feel your love and
it feels brand new every day.

our love will never burn out.
it is an everlasting flame
that even the devil couldn't extinguish.

DEPRESSION IS OPPRESSION
Dylan Starling

Depression is oppression.
It's a deadly hidden message.
Defined by self-hate.
It seals its prisoner's fate.
It holds you captive and throws away the keys .
It stabs and jabs just to see you plea, on your knees.
Inflicting wounds that scar for life.
Destruction is its mother and death is its wife.

You can cry, but it will never acknowledge your screams.
It terrorizes your soul and haunts your dreams.
It sends you false hope through a bottle or pill.
It destroys your goals and inflicts its will.
You can't run, nor can you hide.
By its rules, you will abide.

Open your eyes, or you will be its prey.
It will blur your vision in the most twisted way.
It will seek your destruction and call for your head.
You will lie and wait but never rest in your bed.

Peace will come to those who want peace,
But as long as you feed it, you will see the beast.
You can't run, nor can you hide,
But if you conquer the beast, you will survive.
Prayer and hope can lead the way.
Cling on to every word you pray.
Hope is in truth and hate is in lies.
Pray for your soul and open your eyes.

IN SANE
Margaret Buckner

I haven't been in a while
I haven't been
I haven't

You haven't been yourself in a long time
        been yourself in a long time
                in a long time

It keeps changing every day
It keeps changing
It keeps
    worsening

You keep me sane
But you haven't been yourself
Every day it..
I haven't been sane in a while
Been yourself in a long time
It keeps worsening everyday

ABANDONMENT
Porche Jamar

a shadow.
he was a shadow of the person he used to be
he didn't know who he was anymore
but,
he knew that
once,
he was whole,
and then he wasn't.
he didn't know what had happened
but,
he knew that
she had something to do with it.
she,
the girl,
had walked off with his spirit
slithering through her veins
and,
she hadn't even realized it
all she knew
was that
once,
she was empty,
and then she wasn't.
she didn't know
he had something to do with it.

SIMPLICITY
Raina Verser

I expected thunder-
abrupt, dramatic,
foundation-rumbling thunder-
to explode from my pen
lightning ink striking these lines.

I expected the words to
scorch the page, leaving a trail
of raging flames, metaphors and images
making their presence felt
and savored.

I expected the Muse to rush forth,
Parting the sky and stamping
my feeble work with excellence
to astonish the readers, the critics,
my reverent self.

I expected a grandiose gesture
of Publishers Clearing House proportions,
an envelope in my mailbox clearly labeled:
A chance at ARTISTRY and PASSION!
YOU May Already Be A Poet!

Yet, here I sit, meandering on paper,
attempting to capture
the essence of a bumblebee
that is perched on a morning glory
just beside my feet.

My body is loud
And it ain't the kinda subtle volume voice
Of softly swinging hips that spill from sunken stomach sunkissed silhouette sexy-

No,
My body is electric loud-
4th of july firecrackers loud-
Loud like the girl standing behind you at a concert-
Loud Like when you're tryna take a nap and your mom whips out the vacuum cleaner-
Not to be ignored loud.

And i cannot recount the times i've begged for it to be quiet.
For it to melt into the passing crowd with ease
God, please, grant me this invisibility,
Grant me the ability to feel pretty without trying,
To feel like i'm not drowning inside of my own skin-

Did you know that fat girls are taught shame as our first language?
Taught to shove our hearts in the back with the rack of clothes that actually fit us-
Did you know that we were taught to hate ourselves the same way we were taught how to multiply?
And that's not to say that all girls weren't taught to hate ourselves-
It's just to say that fat girls were never invited to the movement not to.

And i don't like to complain.
But how am i supposed to stay silent
When you tell me that there are weight limits to being human
And i'm just passed the mark-
When everybody thinks they're a doctor as soon as they see me-
On instagram ranting made up statistics about diabetes,
When boys think my body is an invitation
To treat me as the rotten fruit fallen too far from the tree-
He asks me to thank him as he *sinks his teeth into me*-
When i got a phd in being unwanted-

All my life i've been fighting in the battle for my own body
Against a culture that requires perfection-
So this is my declaration of reclaiming.

A reclaiming of my heart-
Where galaxies once grew like sunflowers
Before i learned to hush out my own heartbeat
So that the world could not find it-

A reclaiming
Of my own body
From the shame that has manifested for far too long,
Because this shame was never meant to belong to me,
Because can't nobody take what God has given me-
Because there is beauty in my bounties

I am reclaiming my own body
Because it's mine.
And that in itself is more than enough.

I LOVE WHEN I SHOULDN'T
Kydarra Pope

You told me you loved me
and that there's no end to our "perfect" relationship.
I would love that too, if it were the truth.
Am I your girlfriend, or your pet?
Am I your favorite worthless toy?
Only to play with, and look at to pass the time,
and then be tossed to the ground as if I mean nothing.
My body must be your therapy.
Does my body make you feel better after a long day?
Of being with so many girls?
Or am I the cracked and abandoned sidewalk?
I must be.
You won't even spare me a passing glance,
I'm not even enough for your feet to walk on.
Is my heart your stress ball?
The way you nearly burst it with your anger,
makes me think so.
I must be a joke to you.
The way you laugh in my face when you see the tears in my eyes.
When you walk away from the scars that you have made,
the joy you have taken from me.

Do you even care?

Do you care that I have never left you?
Whenever you needed someone to talk to,
I was here.
But you,
you where never here for me.

GIVE ME A CHANCE

Destionna Cooper

I've been through so much stuff,
it's getting to the point where I'm giving up.
How am I supposed to prove to you
when you don't give me a chance?
How am I supposed to show you
when you put me in situation where I can't?
Are you afraid to let me be?
Can you help me, help you see?
I've been trying for years,
shedding tears,
but I guess you can't hear,
because you weren't close enough to be near.

WHEN THE CHIPS ARE DOWN

Zoë Maddox

"I raise," I said as I slid two bone chips toward the center of the table into the already sizeable pile.

Death smirked as if he had known I would. He simply said call as he threw two similar chips into the pile, matching my bet. I glanced down a little nervously to look at the chips I had left, well chip. At this point I had gambled everything away except my heart. There wasn't much of a chance for me. I had worked myself into a deadly situation because of hubris. Simple as that. And soon, I would have to pay up.

I looked to my cards again. I had a full house, Queens high, a normally good hand, but when playing with death, well, I didn't trust the odds not to fall in his favor. Death studied my face, his expression neutral once again, and as always, impossible to read. I sighed in frustration. If I lost my heart the game was over. But if I didn't put it out there, I would never know if I had missed this chance. The stakes were so high, and at this point, I wasn't sure what was a better gamble.

I made a snap decision and before I could pause to doubt myself any longer I slid the chip to the center of the table. There was no way to retreat now. Death's eyebrows raised slightly, almost as if in surprise, but then he simply nodded and matched my bet again. I couldn't help from biting my lip. I knew I was easy to read in this moment, but it was too late to take any of it back.

I slowly flipped my cards and slid them towards the center of the table. My hands sweating and shaking, I was afraid the cards would go flying. I tried my best to glean something, anything out of Death's face as he studied my cards.

My heart beating faster and harder, I could feel it almost as if it were in my throat, and slowly,

Death showed his hand.

INVISIBLE
Malachi Christian

Who you see
Not what you know
But how
Another layer underneath,
Maybe two or three,
You see, but you'll never know
The reason why people are who they are.
The reason why people do the things they do.
Because you never got a chance to find out.
We see each other but to others
We are invisible.

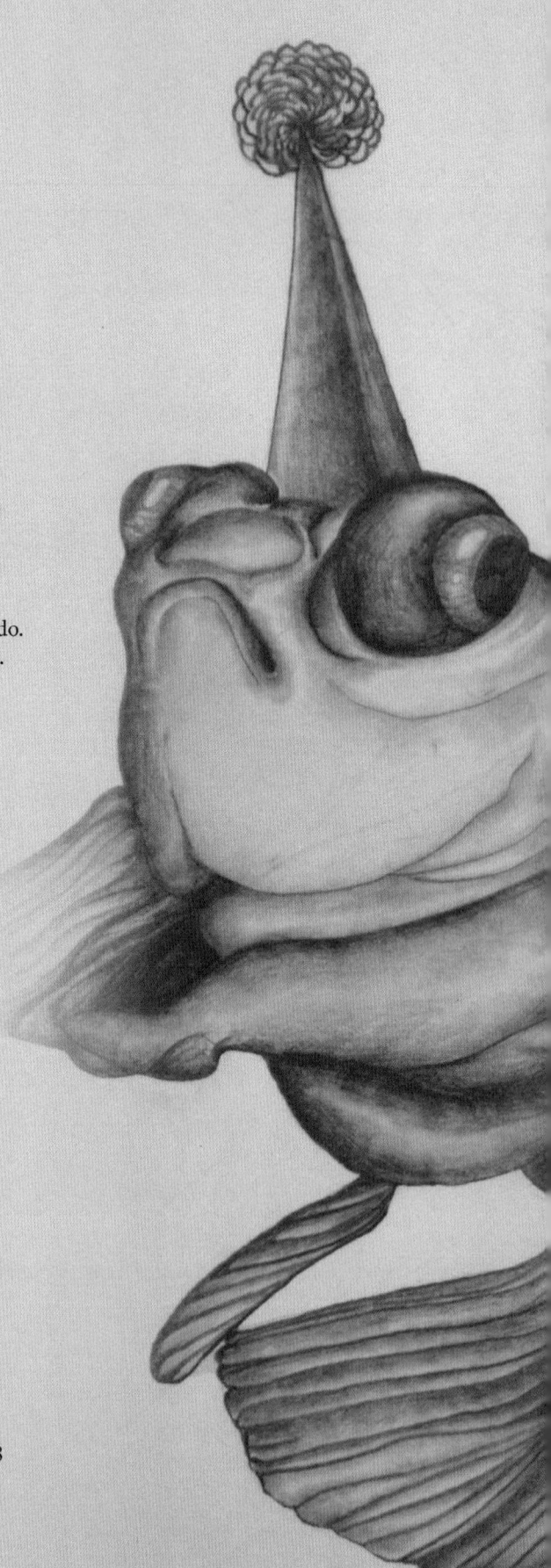

MAKE A WISH
Margaret Buckner

Faulty accusations bled into her
Forgetting their place
As battle scars

The only way back
Was for her to bleed out
Bleed dead

And let her blood
Nourish the seeds
Of dandelions

Make your wish on her memory

GONE
Madison Maine

Have you ever seen your life
flash before your eyes?
I have;
I have as I watched you fall
nine stories
and hit the pavement.
They tried to save you but the damage was done.
You were bent
and broken
and dead.

You held precious memories
now gone
because I hadn't posted them on social media.
You knew me better than most people,
knew my friends, my family.
You saw things the way I did,
even if it took a little convincing.
But now you're gone, and in time,
I will inevitably end up replacing you.

But then again,
the memories lost
were just photos
and you were simply my phone.

TOMATOES
Margaret Buckner

A pool of tomatoes
A boy in a pool of tomatoes
And water lilies
Drowning
Residents walk past
This tightly fought race
Of a boy drowning
In a pool of tomatoes
And water lilies

HOW TO PERFORM THE PERFECT TRADE

Marko Elmore

We've all wanted that specific item that's just out of our reach, whether financially or otherwise. We've always wanted that basketball, or that video game that just came out, or next season's outfit. It tends to nag at us, and we try everything to get to our item. We've taken to working too hard on our job just to get the funds, and never make sure to take care of ourselves and our actual needs. Some of us have died because of this undying want.

But now, we can change that. We can live, and breathe, and be happy with ourselves for once. We can achieve what we've always wanted… for a price. There is a story from the days of old that has appeared on the internet. A list of instructions, if you will. Hidden in the old archives, the instructions sit and wait for someone to read them. It can think, and it can breathe. It knows.

To get what you always wanted, you must have these objects in your possession.
- A flashlight.
- A candle.
- A vehicle (It must be small, but strong enough to withstand the cold).
- A small mirror.
- An item you hold dear to your heart.
- A blunt weapon (like a hammer).

You must not have any people with you for this mission, or you will not get any results. First, you must create a mental map from your dwelling to an abandoned building. Do not use a map or a GPS, as they may change appearance later. Second, park your vehicle in front of your house. Make sure you are alone, and make SURE you do not have any pets near you. Wait until midnight.

Once midnight strikes, proceed to an electrical box and shut down all electronics. Afterwards, slowly maneuver your way through your house. Make sure you are equipped with a flashlight now, as any physical injury will ruin your mission. Make your way over to where your candle is placed, and pick It up. Make your way to a room with a hard floor, like a kitchen, and place the candle down onto the floor.

Next, make your way to a small mirror, and pick that up as well. Finally, pick up a cherished item and pocket it. If it's too big, simply hold it in your arms. Make your way over to the candle, and place the mirror next to the candle. Ignite the candle, and slowly place the mirror over the candle. If you hear nothing besides the crackling of a fire in your house, you did it wrong. However, if you hear a stomp coming from somewhere in your house, make your way out the front door and into your vehicle. Walk, and don't run. If you do run, however, you will not like the end results.

After you make it to your car, begin driving. You must be driving at 50 mph or slower, but never higher than 50 or lower than 25. Make your way to your destination. If you have forgotten where your location is, then drive over 50. This will effectively end your mission without any physical repercussions to you. Just don't return to your house ever again. While driving, you will start to notice that the streets are devoid of traffic and that the sky will be clear, showing stars even if the sky wasn't clear before. Once you reach your destination, quickly exit the car. Sprint towards the abandoned building, and enter. There will be a chance that, if you were too slow when driving or when running, then you will have a third footstep behind you. If you were lucky enough to drive faster, or run faster than your pursuer could catch up to you, then you will hear raspy breathing in your ear, and a cold breeze in the other. Either way, make your way too the second floor if there is one. If there is none, head towards the corner.

When you move, keep your head straight even when you're turning. Do not look left or right. When you reach the corner of the second or first floor, make sure your nose is pressed against the corner. Slowly close your eyes, and relax. It smells your tension and fear. Don't talk, and slowly turn away from the corner. Keep your eyes closed, as it loves the attention. And you will NOT like its attention whatsoever. Even if you do open your eyes, you will not be able to close them again as it's form will either shock you beyond belief, or it is too incomprehensible. Slowly hand the item to the creature. It will take the item, and then you will feel a clawed talon on your hand(s). It will leave an object in your hand, and you will hear faint whispering shortly after. After the whispering stops, it will be safe to open your eyes once more.

It will now be early in the morning, and the streets will be filled once more. Whatever you wanted the most is now rested safely and securely in your hands. Your mission is over, and you are safe to re-enter your home. Just make sure to burn the items before midnight. There's three different catches to this mission.
- You cannot tell anyone about your mission.
- You cannot do the mission again.
- Don't expect a nice afterlife upon death.

I don't have enough time to write the other details, as I myself have just attempted to retry this mission, and I don't think that I will be around much longer.

DON'T BE ASHAMED
Oliver Gemmel

Don't be ashamed because you are different
Because you don't fit in
Because you are bad at sports
Because you aren't pretty enough
Because you aren't perfect
Nobody is
Those people you envy may not be happy
The most successful people weren't popular
They didn't always play sports
They didn't always fit in
They weren't ashamed
You shouldn't be either
The outcasts of the social groups
Can become the most successful

ELASTICITY

Shecoria Akins

You may think I'm dumb. You may think I'm setting myself up for pain again. You may think I'm just going to cry more useless tears and waste more precious time. That's not true. My heart will not break. I've been through too much and hurt too bad. My heart bends now. It may be misshapen for a while but it will snap back. I am invincible. My walls are unconquerable and strong. I am different now, less naive with no expectations. There is no beginning and there is no end but there is right now. Neither my history nor my security matter because if I died right now I'd die with the memory of his skin on mine. I'd die with him and me intertwined as deep as the cells and as shallow as the thoughts. My emotions have been bleached for my own good. I'm clean and bare. I won't get swept up into the wind and blown away like I did before. I just want to feel the breeze. There is no pain when you have no feeling.

I'm not much of a talker anymore.
I don't hold conversations-
I dislike the discomfort of hearing
My own voice dilute empty rooms
And reminding me I'm powerless
I'm not much of a talker anymore.
It's 2017, and I-
I mean we-
Still don't have the power to speak for ourselves.
Rather us,
We fold the laundry
While they ruin-
I mean run-
The world.
In my household,
My mouth was sewn shut
Before I learned to use it as a weapon.
And while my throat aches for the power to speak-
My tired feet pleading for a break from the walk of shame.
I-
I mean we-
Are tired of speaking
Only to remain unheard.

1ST AMENDMENT
Kayla Dunlap

WAR
Daisha Thomas

She took you from me.
She brain-washed you,
letting you think gun powder was your only friend.
Taking memories we once had together,
replacing them with the color red
filled with screams that will never seem to fade away.
She will take the sweetness out of you,
to manipulate it into anger.
That will burrow in you for the rest of your life.
She will make you feel like you've accomplished the world.
Not knowing she took you away from mine.
She took you from place to place,
Letting you think it was an adventure.
An adventure leading to death.
She took you from me,
only to leave us broken.

Excerpt from
MYTH HUNTERS
Ariana Brown

The sound of hearty banter and the smell of alcohol overwhelmed Thane as he stepped into the tavern behind Adina. Men clinked their mugs together and downed their beers as a small band played in a corner. Behind him, Zelpha grinned at the awaiting debauchery and merriment. Adina caught her arm before she could take a step. "Don't get too carried away. We won't be here long."

Zelpha drew her arm away and sketched an exaggerated bow. "Fret not, m'lady. I'll only be having a drink or two… if we're lucky." She gave them a wink, and then she disappeared into the crowd.

Thane wanted to go after her, but Adina shook her head and went in another direction. Not toward the bar, but to the tables nearby. They sat down, Adina going so far as to order beers for the both of them. But they were not here to drink.

After five minutes with neither of them speaking, Thane leaned over and asked, "What, exactly, are we doing here?"

Adina glanced sidelong at him. "Would you believe me if I said I'd wanted to grab a drink?"

"No." Adina hadn't touched her mug since she'd gotten it. All she'd done, really, was watch the activity around her. Part of him wondered if she wanted to join in herself.

But Adina nodded to one table in particular a few tables down. "We're here to hire someone."

Thane hadn't cared to pay any attention to who, exactly, was in the tavern with them. He looked more closely at the men who sat at the table Adina had pointed to. Most men he didn't recognize, but the ones he did…

"General Algeron Kearney?" Thane turned to her, exasperated. "You know he despises you. He'll sooner carve his own eye out than aid your cause."

"I have a feeling he'd find some twisted delight in having one eye." Adina said thoughtfully as she lifted her mug to finally take a drink from it.

"This isn't a joke, Dina." Thane shook his head. "He'll never help you."

"Well then," Adina stood, mug in hand, "I suppose it's a good thing I'm not here for him." Before Thane could further object, she sauntered over to Kearny's table, Thane close on her heels. Kearney and his men were too busy laughing and drinking to notice them until Adina spoke. "I would've thought you and your men would have better things to do on your leave, General."

Kearney looked up as he set his mug on the table, a wicked smile on his lips. "Dina, dear!" His voice was mocking venom, and his words were that of a lover. Thane bristled, but Adina's face was impassive. "I would've thought you'd have better things to do than follow me around," he shrugged, "but I suppose not, being the king's pet and all. And Thane," he turned his attention to him, smirking, "still her loyal lap dog, I take it?"

Thane ground his teeth together. Before he could snap a retort, Adina said, her tone bored, "The king dispatched me on an important mission, and I find myself in need of one of your crew members. Otherwise, I would not be slumming with the vermin."

That comment wiped the smirk right off of Kearney's face. He snarled for a moment before his face became unreadable and he leaned back in his chair. "None of my men will aid your cause. Even if I gave them permission to leave, they would not disgrace themselves by joining you."

"I don't want your men. They're all raging drunks anyway." If looks could start a fire, Adina's ashes would burn from the glares of Kearney's men, but Adina didn't even glance at them. She simply pointed to a girl sitting beside Kearney, and the girl's hazel eyes widened. "I want her."

Thane hadn't even noticed the girl until Adina had pointed her out; she was so small compared to the muscled men surrounding her, and she shrank even smaller at all the attention that was drawn to her.

For a moment the men at the table were quiet, then they all burst into laughter. "You want a poor healer girl as your first recruit?"

"She's not our first recruit," Adina shrugged. "But if she's of no value to you, then there's no trouble."

Kearney narrowed his eyes. "Perhaps she is, if you want her so badly."

"I simply need a healer."

"There are many healers in the kingdom. Why seek mine?"

Adina smirked, the first crack in her emotionless shield. "I enjoy taking things from you."

A muscle in Kearney's jaw twitched. "I'll need another healer."

"I'm sure the king would be happy to provide you with one." The mention of his Majesty was a threat, a jab to remind him who was the higher ranking officer, to show she was growing tired of their argument.

Kearney was silent for a moment, then he turned to the girl. "You have my permission to leave with General Adina Armstrong."

The girl stared at Kearney for a moment, as if in disbelief, then looked to Adina, Thane, and back at Kearney.

"Well, come on then," Adina said, almost encouragingly, "we haven't got all day." Adina turned and walked away, Thane following her, expecting the girl to follow.

Thankfully, she did so without hesitation.

WOMANHOOD
Daisha Thomas

I am a woman.
I am the roaring sea,
Not the calm waters.
I am the harsh hurricane winds,
Not the blissful breeze.
I am the tormenting blizzard,
Not the soft snowfall.

I am a woman,
I am strong.
A warrior,
I am wise.
An achiever,
I am demanding.
I will be respected.

I am a woman.
A woman who still develops confidence.
I am a woman.
A woman who still struggles.
I am a woman.
A woman who wants all women to come together.
Because we,
We are women.

YOUR EYES
Bella Garbeil

Alright, so, Little Darling with the pretty brown eyes
Who said your eyes aren't pretty?
All those love songs about blue eyed girls, green eyed girls,
Forget 'em.

Little Darlin', you got eyes like maple leaves in autumn breeze,
Like Angel Oaks that stand older than the houses we had built
On their soil-
Got eyes richer than Earth Goddesses grow their flowers in.

Little Darling, you got eyes like the gold that forms in the ground
Deep beneath our feet-
You got eyes like obsidian, that gleams blue against the light
Like the topaz us human folk dig so hard and so fast to find.

Little Darlin'-
Make no mistake, those girls are pretty, those girls that come in
Jewel tones, and tea leaves, and rainy clouds fresh from the English Sky.
But remember, Little Darling,

That you hold the Earth in your irises-
And never you forget.

MONSTER IN THE BED
Natalie Roberts

this is for my friend emily-
or maybe for my cousin taylor,
or maybe for leah
or mary
or amiyah-

isn't it strange
the way girls have learned to whisper their own horror stories
under blanketed darkness-
as if the tv in the background
could bury the screams caught like a bird in our throats-

Mama, there's a Problem-

and isn't it funny
the way
all of our stories start to bleed together-
i'm listening to moriah tell me how he was there when she woke up-
and my stomach is sick because i've seen this movie before-
i know how it ends-
i can't help but think about how
elise was drunk but he didn't care when-
lilly was scared and he kept going so-
amber said no a hundred times but-
moriah laughs as if to push it back under the rug
where it can grow mold and fester inside of her-

rotten fruit in her Garden of Eden-

Mama, Something has happened-

and no one will ask why-

why are we breeding boys into monsters-
with hands like teeth that take,
rather than build-
they're stealing more from us than you realize-
why did they give us makeup as if it were battle paint-
and drop us off at the mall as if sending us to war-
why did our mothers tell us about pimples and periods
but never about this-
surely they remember how blood drips down roses
like tears-
why is silence beaten into us until we can no longer remember the sound of our own voice screaming?
why does no one ask why?

Mama, i feel like i can't Breathe

i learned how to be a doctor
long before i learned how to be a student or a writer or a girlfriend-
stitching up the distances between the pieces of my friends broken hearts,
sewing healing into the palms of warriors-
with mascara-stained cheeks-

Mama, he took too Much-

boys laugh together on boulevards of immaculate white sun-
while girls form friendships under starlight-
hands clasped tight under inky blue sky-
comparing battle scars from our nights spent
batting off boys with bad breath,
hoping against hope that we'll be able to save each other,
this time.

Mama, i'm scared there's Nothing left of me.

SERENDIPITY
Porche Jamar

and,
they say that we are the lucky ones
because,
we don't have to go through life
constantly looking over our shoulders
and we decide whether we wish to speak or remain silent.
but,
don't they realize,
that we have it just as bad?
can they not see that we, too,
are trapped?
they say that we are the lucky ones.
because our chains are not visibly wrapped around us like theirs,
and the naked eye cannot see the ways in which we are disrespected.
because,
it is subtle.
it's in the way that they ask you if you had been drinking.
or if you were dressed appropriately.
or if you might have given any hints that you wanted something.
even when you didn't.
still,
they say that we are the lucky ones
but,
the truth is,
we have it just as bad.

WHAT IT MEANS TO BE A WOMAN
Iauniss Smith

People think that women are these creatures, creatures that obtain mixed emotions and can display all of them at once. People ask, "What does it mean to be a woman?" To be a woman means to hold your head up high, not with a cocky attitude, but with pride. To be a woman means to feel free spirited, spreading your wings as far as they can go and soaring through the open air, however keeping in mind that your wings can, and will, be damaged.

To be a woman means to keep everything in balance while it's all falling apart. Crying when no one's looking and getting up in the morning, acting as if everything is perfect.

To be a woman means to be in constant competition with your enemy, my enemy, our enemy: other women. To get knocked back down before you've had the chance to get up; is that not what we women do? Having actions describe us, words define us, what we wear and how we speak mold us, the memories we hold and things we've been through… that truly defines a woman.

To show strength in times of weakness to sew our words together and make them like silk, to be graceful and eloquent; all these components mixed together are women. Sacrifice is encrypted in our DNA, giving others what we don't have or what we'll never have a chance at getting.

Oh how we are held to such high expectations, having little to no time to achieve them. Oh how men call us stubborn when we reject an option- or is it that we refuse to take no for an answer?

Oh how we have come so far in this world, facing adversities, overcoming inequality, and stepping over discrimination just because we are the opposite sex- we are women. Oh how we've been such a great factor in this world: from being the birth of the nation to sacrificing everything we have under God's creation.

Oh how we could be so much more than what we are credited for. Oh the mysteries that creep within us, the dangers that arise in us, the love that makes us. Oh the demand we receive when we walk into a room… oh how we could be so much more than what we are credited for.

Diamonds in the rough, roses with thorns, peaceful wars, beautiful nightmares, and precious monsters. That is what we are; allowing life to have an effect on us, change after change after change.

This is what it means to be a woman.

TOGETHER WE CAN
Siouxann Juber

Together we stand,
Together we fall.
We unite as one
But we do not show it at all.

We do not show that we care about the people around us,
We do not show that we want to protect them.
We only show the hatred and disappointment towards others.
We only reveal negativity never positivity.

The human race can be cruel, but also can be kind.
Stop the fighting,
Stop the hate.
Stop saying, "You mean nothing to me,"
Start saying "I will always be here for you."

Throughout the years, I have seen and heard from the good,
And the bad.
I have heard them spit out their lies and spin their tales of spiteful truths.
I have seen the darkness in some, but
Also the light beneath the void.

Do not be someone who brings down the stars,
Who hold the dreams of people who look up at them at night,
And say, "This is who I want to be."
Be the one who helps people catch those stars.

I know you and I are both one of them dangling in the sky,
Make this world a better place.
I hope my words do not go to waste,
And that they are not just considered to be hot air.

I want them to mean something,
And hopefully make someone realize
That being cruel is wrong.
And being kind is right.

Together we stand,
Together we fall.
Finally,
We unite as one.

Excerpt from
THE UNTITLED
Ben Watts

"I'm sorry," I whispered to her, "I'm so sorry. I made a mistake, and I don't deserve forgiveness, but I'm still here standing before you."

She remained quiet. Her silence was more painful than anything she could've said. Because if she spoke, I'd have a definitive answer. I wouldn't be standing here, blubbering and begging for forgiveness, when there was none to be given. I could move on.

Her brain was obviously working. I knew she was torn on the idea. On one hand, I admit that I screwed up, and I was willing to come back. On the other, I had broken her heart, and was begging desperately for a second chance. But silence continued to reign.

It blanketed me, and smothered me. I didn't want silence, I wanted an answer, I wanted to know if I could amend the mistakes I had made. Apparently, I couldn't.

She closed the front door, and I hung my head low, defeated. I didn't know if she even wanted to be around me, anymore. She more than likely just wanted me to fall off the edge of a cliff, so she wouldn't have to deal with me, anymore.

SHACKLES
Ariahna Battle

She was imprisoned in his eyes, his lips, and his smile,
He was imprisoned in her curves, her chocolate eyes, her laugh,
They fit together like puzzle pieces, to the naked eye
But the problems were underlying,
As well as overwhelming
He feared she would find another to love
Of course, she feared the same
Although, she always said she could
And
She would
She would never, and he knew she wouldn't
Although, he would get angry and threaten to put a hand on her
He would never,
In fact,
He would never lay a finger on her
He cherished her,
She cherished him,
They were imprisoned together

GRAVITY
Colby Meeks

You asked me when I first fell in love with you.

"It wasn't our first date," I answered, "and it wasn't our second, either.

"It was the night at the party, the night you told me you didn't believe in gravity. I asked how many drinks you had and you told me none, that you didn't drink. I laughed, until I realized you weren't joking.

"You told me if gravity was real, the Earth wouldn't be beautiful. All the trees would fall down and the sunflowers would grow like snakes, slithering along the ground.

"I opened my mouth to tell you that plants are just stronger, stronger than the gravity that holds us down but I stopped,

"Something about what you said was beautiful. I realized my own blind acceptance of everything I was told. I still believe in gravity, like how I believe in you and like how I believe in us,"

When I finished telling the story, I looked at your silhouette of a figure in the dark room and realized that you were asleep. I threw an old blanket over you and thanked God that gravity was real because it meant you would stay right there in my hoodie, that you wouldn't float away from me. I think I fell in love with you all over again that night, just like I do every night.

MY LOVE
David Vieyra

You said thank you,
You said thank you
Oh, my dear love you did not have to
You did not have to
Not with me
Besides I can see it your eyes
They lose me like the sea
Cause with you there's so much I would do
Cause my love shines brighter that the sun
With you that's all I ever need
So, will you dance with me tonight
Under the starry sky
And please
No thank you's not now
Just dance the night aways
Let us dance in your dreams
Let us dance, let us dance
Let us dance the nights away

HOME
Zoë Maddox

I choose the night

Because sometimes the cool allure of darkness

Is warmer than the heat of the sun

Whose intensity can sometimes burn too hot for damaged skin

And

Because sometimes the sun is too bright, too harsh

And the caress of darkness that keeps the nightmares away

Is better than anything the sun could ever give

And

Dreamers with shining stars above their heads

Are a better home than a garden of thorns

No matter how pretty the roses are

Under the care of the sun

So

I choose the night

And

The safety I find in its depths

THIN ICE
Shercoria Akins

When you die, your body becomes cold.
Everything inside of you is frozen inside.
Death is cold.

I shiver in the cold snow with my red scarf wrapped around my neck and my fingers balled up in my gloves. I laugh as you serenade me and spin on your ice skates.

Round and round, a perfect figure eight on the ice. I can't skate but I love to watch you glide. I stop shivering as you smile because it makes me feel a sweet warmth in my stomach, like hot chocolate by the fireplace.

Crack. You fall under. I fall over. I run and I slip. You flail and you sink. You're no longer smiling, and I'm no longer warm.

AT THE WOMEN'S MARCH
Maya Glenn

There are certain moments you don't begin to expect will define you. At the beginning of 2017, following President Trump's inauguration, I attended the Women's March in Washington D.C. I knew that it would be something that would stick with me forever, but I never could have guessed the impact that it had not only on me, but on an entire nation of individuals.

Immediately I noticed the amount of people, hundreds and hundreds of thousands, crowding the National Mall with barely any space in between each person. While I expected there to be a majority women, there were many men marching as well. There were people of every color and ethnicity, every religion and set of beliefs, young and old. Everyone was packed together like I've never seen before, yet everyone was comfortable and kind. What at first seemed to be a large protest of President Trump, soon occurred to me was a gathering of people in our nation that demanded rights and respect. It was amazing to me that in a crowd of that many people, there was no violence or angered yelling.

As I marched with all these people, I began to realize that my voice did matter. My whole life I've thought that since I was just one person with no real influence, as well as a child, that my voice didn't matter. The idea that this many people traveled from all over the country, just so their voices could be heard was amazing to me. I felt empowered, and I'm sure others did too. We, as a movement didn't just support the rights of women either, we represented minorities (Black Lives Matter, Muslim Culture, etc.) and we threw our voices in the faces of people that did not want to see us succeed.

In the few hours that I marched, I felt a huge shift in my life. Suddenly I mattered, my voice mattered, all these people who never felt like anything mattered. This was a moment that defined who I have and will become. I've felt more like a leader in my community, in my school, and even in my home. The Women's March showed me that I can, and will, make a difference.

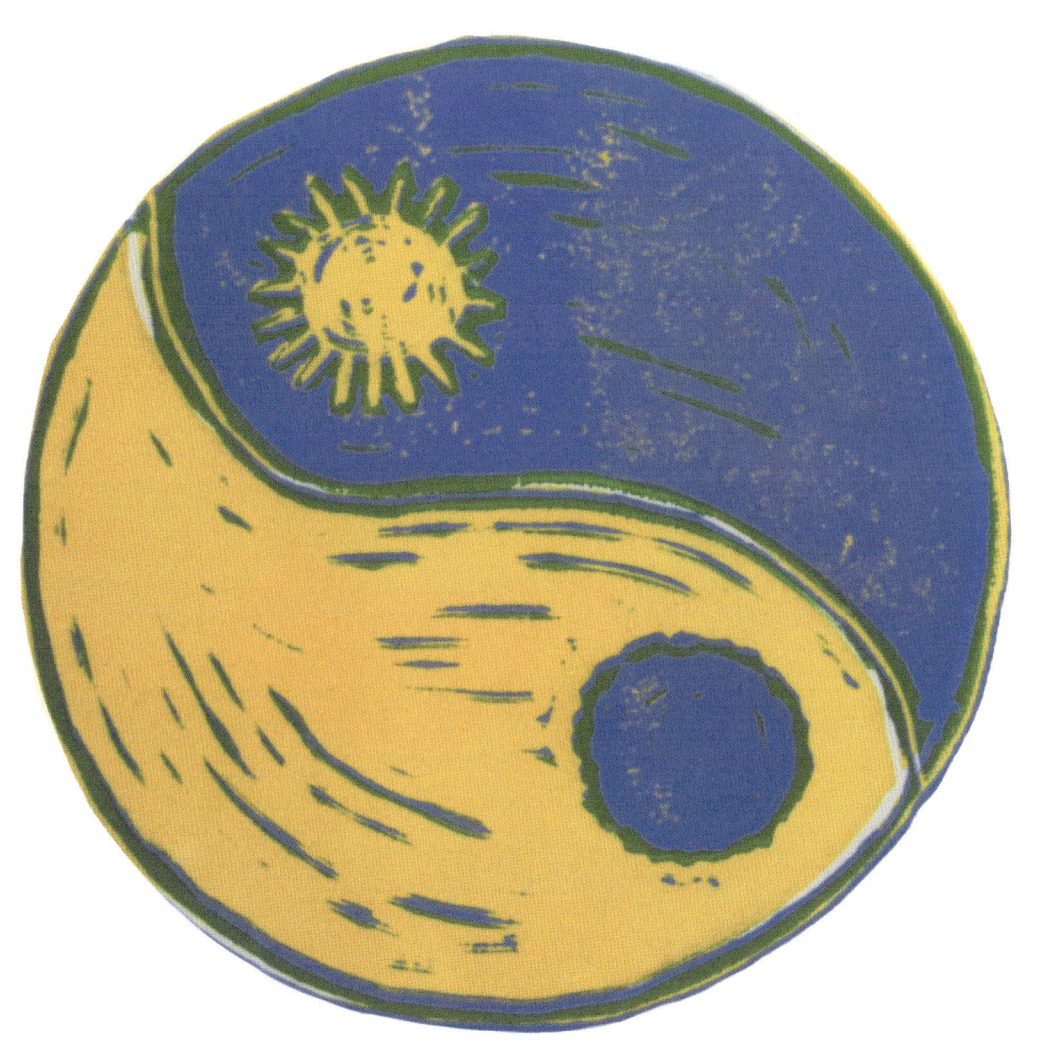

FEARFUL LOVER
Suzãnne Drouilhet

for some reason
i've almost given up on love
and everything like that
i want someone to hold and cherish
but i'm afraid of commitment
it's not that i'm afraid to love
someone forever
i'm just worried they'll turn into a monster
or that i'll neglect the flower of love again
i'm so young
i shouldn't be so worried
about falling in love

"I remember the night," he spoke in a low tone, "you had called me crying."

I shifted around in bed, and turned over to face him. The streetlight shining through the window casted a faint orange outline on his face.

"Why was I crying?" I asked. I laid my head on his chest as I listened for his voice. I could recall the amount of alcohol I had that night, but I couldn't remember the call. He wrapped his arm around my bare torso and pulled me closer to him.

"You were drunk. I asked what was the matter, and you said," he inhaled deeply, "you said you were afraid. And when I asked why, you said because you were falling in love with me."

THE CALL I DON'T REMEMBER
Kayla Dunlap

MORE THAN HUMAN
Keira Folsom

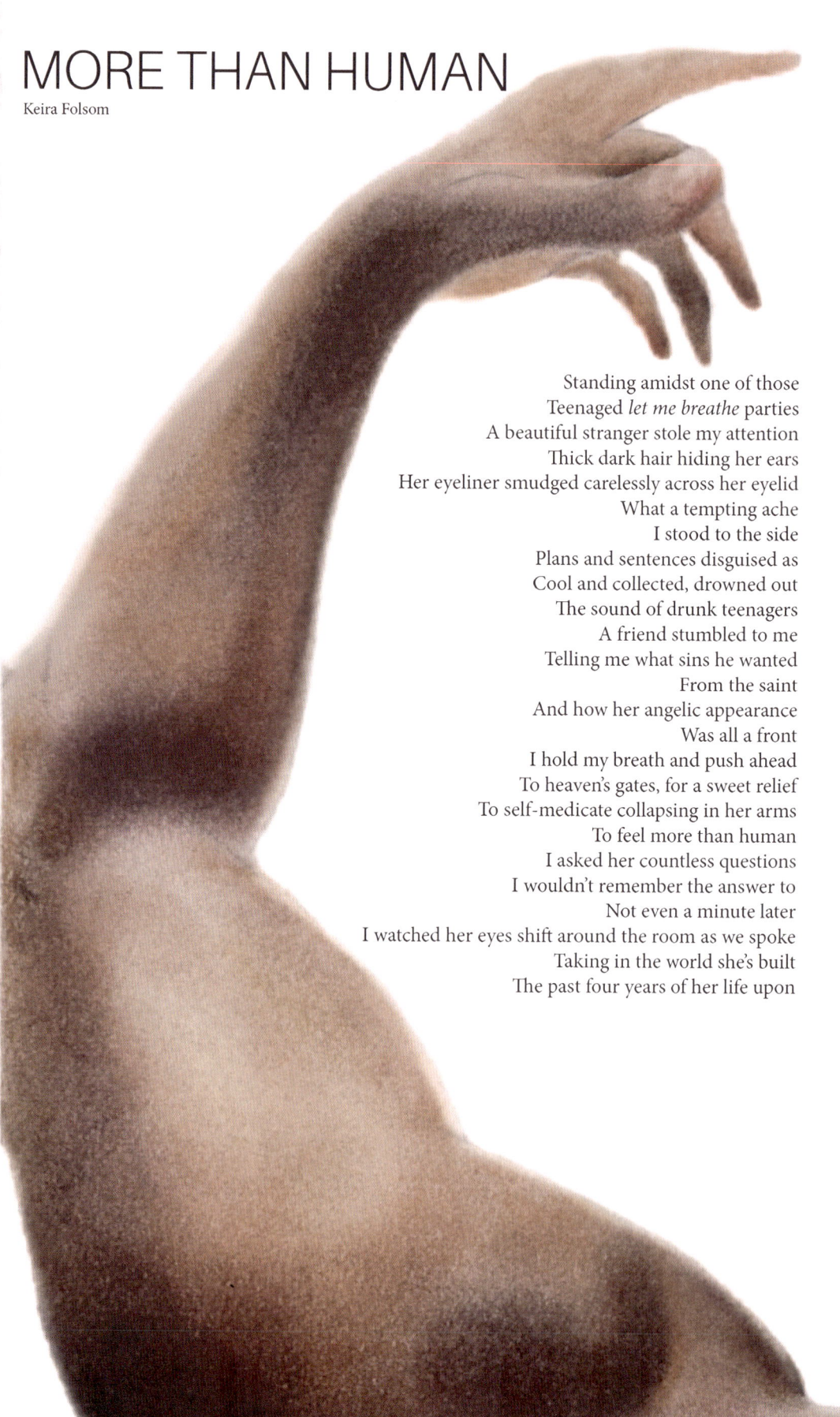

Standing amidst one of those
Teenaged *let me breathe* parties
A beautiful stranger stole my attention
Thick dark hair hiding her ears
Her eyeliner smudged carelessly across her eyelid
What a tempting ache
I stood to the side
Plans and sentences disguised as
Cool and collected, drowned out
The sound of drunk teenagers
A friend stumbled to me
Telling me what sins he wanted
From the saint
And how her angelic appearance
Was all a front
I hold my breath and push ahead
To heaven's gates, for a sweet relief
To self-medicate collapsing in her arms
To feel more than human
I asked her countless questions
I wouldn't remember the answer to
Not even a minute later
I watched her eyes shift around the room as we spoke
Taking in the world she's built
The past four years of her life upon

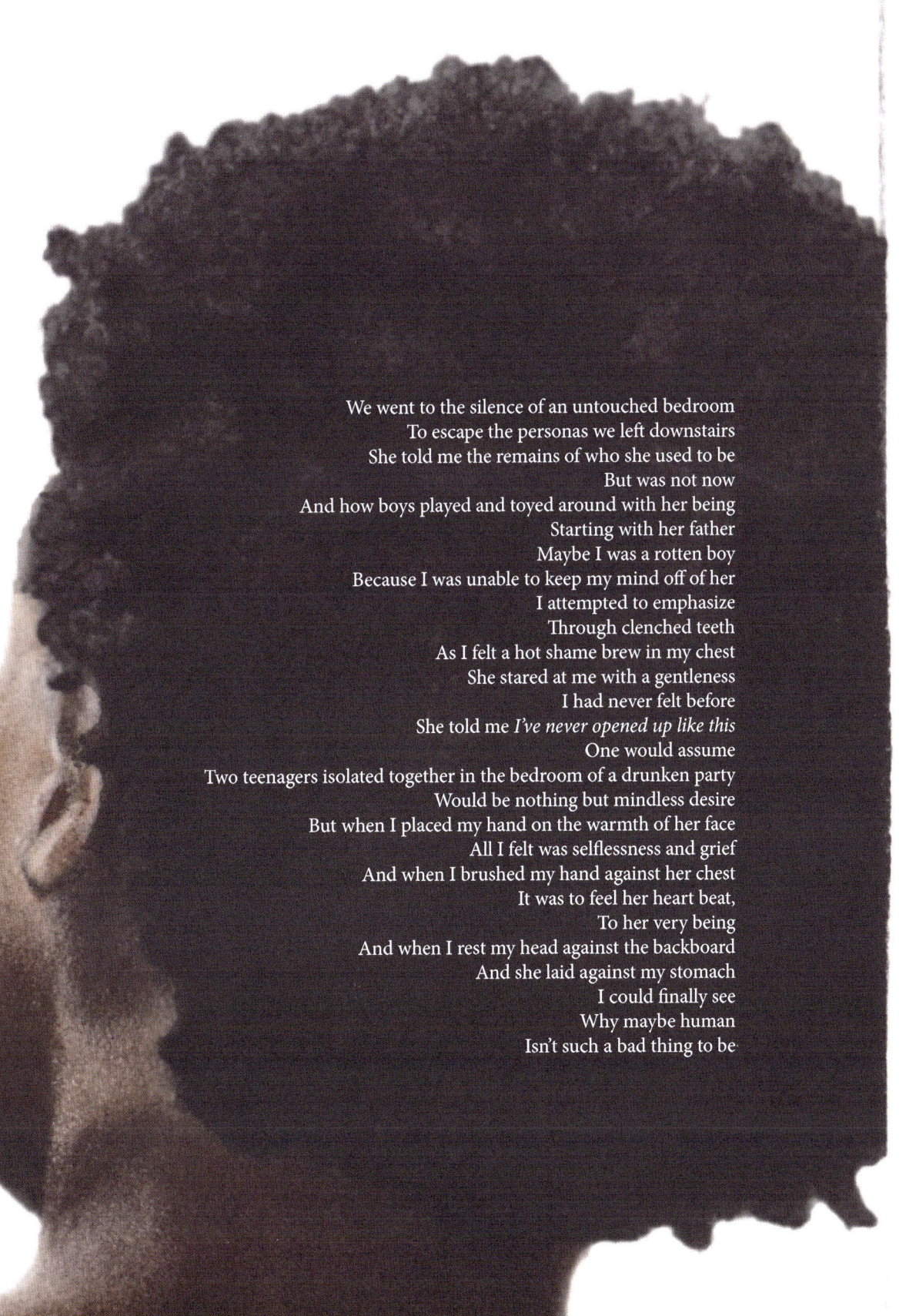

We went to the silence of an untouched bedroom
To escape the personas we left downstairs
She told me the remains of who she used to be
But was not now
And how boys played and toyed around with her being
Starting with her father
Maybe I was a rotten boy
Because I was unable to keep my mind off of her
I attempted to emphasize
Through clenched teeth
As I felt a hot shame brew in my chest
She stared at me with a gentleness
I had never felt before
She told me *I've never opened up like this*
One would assume
Two teenagers isolated together in the bedroom of a drunken party
Would be nothing but mindless desire
But when I placed my hand on the warmth of her face
All I felt was selflessness and grief
And when I brushed my hand against her chest
It was to feel her heart beat,
To her very being
And when I rest my head against the backboard
And she laid against my stomach
I could finally see
Why maybe human
Isn't such a bad thing to be

i remember when i sat at that bar,
thoughts in my head colliding like car crashes—
i was in the process of emptying my bones and my wallet—
i just got paid that morning.
i was already floating on the stool,
but not far enough
because you were still crossing streets in my mind
picking at the last garden on the corner of the crashes;
calendulas and canna lilies
lightly decorating my frontal lobe—
i wanted you gone.

later that night,
i went back home
to my stagnant four walls.
lines of poetry on the knives,
ready to tear you apart like nobody else could;
lines of thrill on the table,
cutting edges of my desolation—
just a cheap trip
to somewhere you aren't.

it's easier to not think about you
because you take too much from me
and give nothing in return.
in my body,
i have nothing.
you took myself from me,
and i was so vulnerable,
i sold the inner workings in my bones for
a pack of cigarettes—
i've emptied them dry.

i'm only filling voids you created
but i'm running out of sources,
if i leave right now—
if i'm off this earth in the morning,
what would you do with the parts you took?

VAMPIRES SMOKE MENTHOLS
Kayla Dunlap

They say that there are 5 stages of you.

They speak of you the way Algebra speaks of graphs, as if i could calculate your slope, as if you had a beginning and an end. they tell me that you are a six-month program that i can graduate from, earn my credentials of loss- get my certificate and pin it to my sleeve, wear it proudly as i step into the sunlight of acceptance-"I have grieved"

And know of young poets who write of you so appetizingly, the appetizer to the main course where we gorge on taboo topics- unhealthy minds who love pain far too much- they write you beautifully, and i don't know why.

Because you, you are the mold that grows dark like seeds in the pits of the cups on my nightstand, i turn my back on you and fall headlong into half-sleep with too many dreams turning in my mind, you

are a mountain of laundry that i don't bother to climb, all i'll find at the top is an open space full of her absence-

you are the tears which i pulled back inside of myself until it burned, because crying meant there was something to cry about-and this brokenness made my bones tired- and i guess i got the steps all mixed up because depression was supposed to come after denial, wasn't it?

but don't take this the wrong way, I mean, hey, you're not all bad. You were with me when no one else was, steady as everything else was shifting, there were days when you, were my best friend. Laughed with me late into the night, I opened my arms for you because sometimes, your presence feels like hers. You gave me something to drown in when the air was all too much-

brought me memories like offerings as if to say "I'm sorry"-
You, grief, are not the wound, you're just the scarring, our broken minds trying to salvage everything we've lost, trying to wrap ourselves around the reality that someone who was here- present-

breathing- laughing with us is just- not.
You are not the wildfire, you're just the land it left behind. The memories of wildflowers in a barren space,

Flowers grow, even on scarred land.
You are the reminder that we can grow too.

We can grow too.

GRIEF
Natalie Roberts

Made in the USA
Columbia, SC
13 March 2018